****
LITTLE
BOOK OF
JEWISH
APPETIZERS
****

LITTLE
BOOK
OF
JEWISH

APPETIZERS

LEAH KOENIG

Photographs by **LINDA PUGLIESE**

CHRONICLE BOOKS

****

The Little Book series is a collection of thematic Jewish cookbooks that will be published serially. Each book will include a bite-size collection of meticulously curated and globally inspired Jewish recipes. Packaged in slim, gorgeously designed books, a single volume—or the whole series—will fit perfectly on and enhance any cookbook shelf.

****

Text copyright © 2017 by Leah Koenig.
Photographs copyright © 2017 by Chronicle Books LLC.
All rights reserved. No part of this book may be reproduced
in any form without written permission from the publisher.
Library of Congress Cataloging-in-Publication Data available.
ISBN 978-1-4521-5913-3
Manufactured in China

Designed by Vanessa Dina
Photographs by Linda Pugliese
Prop styling by Paige Hicks
Food styling by Carrie Purcell
Typesetting by Frank Brayton

Chronicle books and gifts are available at special quantity discounts to corporations, professional associations, literacy programs, and other organizations. For details and discount information, please contact our premiums department at corporatesales@chroniclebooks.com or at 1-800-759-0190.

10 9 8 7 6 5 4 3 2 1

Chronicle Books LLC
680 Second Street
San Francisco, California 94107
www.chroniclebooks.com

To
Max Elisha

INTRODUCTION

Jewish cuisine is filled with showstopping dishes. Think of a bowl of golden, fat-glistening matzo ball soup, a towering pastrami sandwich streaked with mustard, or the grandeur of a platter of Persian rice, with its gloriously crisp and bronzed cap. These foods are celebrations. They are events. They are meals unto themselves. But behind every great dinner—or more precisely, before it—there's a great appetizer.

In Yiddish, the word for appetizer is *forspeis* (pronounced FOR-shpice). Rooted in the German phrase for "before food," *forspeisn* are small offerings—a slice of gefilte fish, say, or a bit of chopped liver—served before the main course to quiet the belly's rumblings and set the stage for the meal.

Middle Eastern and Mediterranean cuisines share a related, though usually more flamboyantly executed, concept called mezze. A typical Sephardi Shabbat dinner is precluded by an overwhelming parade of spreads, vegetables, and small plates. From the tangy red pepper, pomegranate, and walnut dip called muhammara to pickled turnips and smoky charred eggplant drizzled with tahini, the selection can swell to more than a dozen distinct offerings on a single table.

Despite my attempts to exercise a little restraint, I find it almost impossible not to fill up on the appetizer course. But I'm okay with that. Regardless of what masterpieces the cook has up his or her sleeve, these first dishes are the inevitable highlight of the meal. They are like the comedian who warms up the crowd before the featured act and ends up stealing the show.

Beyond the dinner table, Jewish cuisine is filled with countless other little nibbles, snacks, party fare, and between-meal foods. These dishes—a still-warm knish or piece of strudel tucked into a child's hand on the way out the door, a plate of buttercream-rich hummus split with a friend for an afternoon nosh, or a perfect bite of spicy, Sephardi-style meatball plucked from a platter at a cocktail party— are a compelling reminder that food doesn't need to be big and bold to be magnificent.

The *Little Book of Jewish Appetizers*, the first of Chronicle Books' Little Book cookbook series, is my ode to Jewish cuisine's smallest delights. The recipes span the globe from Morocco (Moroccan Orange and Black Olive Salad, page 36) and Manhattan (Smoked Trout Canapés, page 51) to Russia (Mushroom Piroshki, page 99) and Rome (Fried Artichoke Hearts, page 73) to capture the tradition's ultimate appetizers. They include both classic dishes (Chopped Egg and Caramelized Onion Spread, page 12; Lahmajun, page 113; Perfect Tzatziki, page 33) as well as creative spins on traditional flavors (Borscht Crostini, page 46; and Shiitake and Scallion Falafel, page 75). As a collection, I hope they delight, surprise, and like any good starter should, whet the appetite for more.

* *

A Note About Serving Sizes
Several of the dishes in *Little Book of Jewish Appetizers* could technically be enjoyed as the main course. Please keep in mind that all of the serving sizes included with the recipes assume they are being eaten as a starter or snack and that additional courses will follow.

* *

CHAPTER 1

FRESH, TOASTED, PICKLED

This chapter is filled with silky spreads, fresh vegetable dishes, briny pickles, and full-flavored crostini that will start dinner or a party off on the right foot. Scoop everything up with one of the suggestions for Next-Level Dippers on page 22.

Chopped Egg and Caramelized Onion Spread

SERVES 6 TO 8

There's egg salad, and then there's chopped egg and onions. The former is wonderful—a creamy delicatessen favorite. But the latter, while lesser known, is an under-cover, Ashkenazi superstar. The secret lies with the onions, which are caramelized before being folded into the coarsely chopped eggs, adding incomparable depth and sweetness.

On a trip to Budapest a few years back, I was delighted to find chopped egg and onion on the menu at the modern Jewish-Hungarian restaurant, Macesz Bistro. They called the dish Jewish-style eggs and softened their onions in savory duck schmaltz (rendered poultry fat). In my take, I add a shallot to the mix for a bit of nuance and keep the mayonnaise to a bare minimum—enough to bind everything together, while still allowing the incredible flavors to shine through. Serve on toasted rye, hearty brown bread, a slab of challah, or with crackers. It also makes a delicious dip for crudités.

8 EGGS
3 TBSP VEGETABLE OIL OR SCHMALTZ
2 MEDIUM ONIONS, FINELY CHOPPED
1 MEDIUM SHALLOT, FINELY CHOPPED
KOSHER SALT AND FRESHLY GROUND BLACK PEPPER
3 TBSP MAYONNAISE
1 TSP SWEET PAPRIKA

1. Place the eggs in a medium saucepan. Cover with water by 2 in [5 cm] and set the pan, uncovered, over high heat. When the water boils, turn off the heat, cover the pan, and let sit for 18 minutes. Drain the eggs and rinse well under cold water to stop the cooking process. Peel the eggs, cut them in half, and set aside.

2. Meanwhile, heat the oil in a large skillet set over medium heat. Add the onions and shallot, cover, and cook until they begin to soften, 5 to 10 minutes. Uncover the pan, season with a little salt, and stir in 1 Tbsp water. Continue to cook, stirring often, until the onion and shallot take on a golden color with some crispy edges, 5 to 10 minutes more. Remove from the heat and set aside to cool slightly.

3. Combine the cooked eggs and half of the onion mixture in a food processor and pulse a few times to break everything up. Be careful not to overprocess—the mixture should look textured and fluffy, not smooth or pasty. Transfer to a medium bowl. Gently fold in the mayonnaise, paprika, and reserved onion mixture. Season with salt and pepper to taste. Serve warm or cold, and store leftovers in an airtight container in the refrigerator for up to 3 days.

Vegetarian Chopped Liver with Shallots

SERVES 8 TO 10

Chopped chicken liver (*gehakte leber* in Yiddish) was so iconic and central to the Eastern European Jewish diet, that American Jews crafted a way to eat it with dairy as well as meat meals. The meatless version, known as either vegetarian chopped liver or mock chopped liver, rose to prominence in the scores of dairy restaurants that once slung blintzes, cheesecake, and borscht with sour cream on New York City's Lower East Side.

According to *Arthur Schwartz's Jewish Home Cooking: Yiddish Recipes Revisted*, mid-twentieth-century vegetarian "liver" recipes were made with canned peas or canned string beans mashed up, flavored with copious amounts of fried onions, and thickened with ground walnuts and Manischewitz Tam Tams crackers. The version at the most famous New York City dairy restaurant, Ratner's, used ground-up cooked lentils to reach a faux-meaty texture and taste and contained a secret ingredient: a spoonful of peanut butter! I prefer to start with hearty kidney beans and amp them up with several umami-packed additions, like cremini mushrooms and sautéed shallots. A few hard-boiled eggs whirred into the food processor add richness to the creamy bean base. Serve the spread with crackers for dipping or layer it on challah or rye bread.

3 EGGS

3 TBSP VEGETABLE OIL

¾ LB [340 G] SHALLOTS, THINLY SLICED INTO RINGS

KOSHER SALT AND FRESHLY GROUND BLACK PEPPER

½ LB [225 G] CREMINI MUSHROOMS, CLEANED, STEMMED, AND CHOPPED

1 TBSP BROWN SUGAR

¼ CUP [30G] CHOPPED WALNUTS

ONE 15-OZ [425-G] CAN KIDNEY BEANS, DRAINED

2 TBSP MAYONNAISE

1 TBSP SWEET PAPRIKA

1 TSP ONION POWDER

1. Place the eggs in a small pot. Cover with water by 2 in [5 cm] and set the pot, uncovered, over high heat. When the water boils, turn off the heat, cover the pot, and let sit for 18 minutes. Drain the eggs and rinse well under cold water to stop the cooking process. Peel the eggs, cut them into quarters, and set aside.

2. Meanwhile, heat the oil in a skillet set over medium heat. Add the shallots and a pinch of salt, cover, and cook until softened and lightly browned, about 10 minutes. Uncover the pan, add the mushrooms and brown sugar, and continue to cook, stirring occasionally, until deeply browned and most of the mushrooms' liquid evaporates, about 10 minutes. Remove from the heat and set aside to cool slightly.

3. Combine the cooked eggs, the shallot and mushroom mixture, walnuts, kidney beans, mayonnaise, paprika, onion powder, and a generous amount of salt and pepper in a food processor and pulse until smooth, scraping down the sides of the processor bowl as necessary. Transfer to a medium bowl, cover, and refrigerate for at least 2 hours or overnight to let the flavors meld. Serve cold or at room temperature. Store leftovers in an airtight container in the refrigerator for up to 3 days.

Smoky Sweet Potato Hummus

SERVES 6 TO 8

A lot of strange and not-so-wonderful things have been done to hummus over the decades. As the Middle Eastern chickpea and tahini dip started to gain notoriety in America in the 1980s and '90s, variations on the theme began to show up on supermarket shelves. It started innocently with combinations like roasted red pepper and pesto hummus. But more recently, the trend has gone haywire, giving birth to ill-advised concoctions like ranch and even pizza-flavored hummus.

I am all for making innovative tweaks to a traditional recipe as long as I can still identify the original dish's soul. This take on hummus retains the dip's structural integrity—chickpeas, tahini, garlic—while elevating its flavor profile. Roasted sweet potato adds a touch of sweetness and a sunset color. Meanwhile, a hint of smoked paprika lends woodsy depth that I find completely captivating. Serious spice lovers can dial up the amount of ground cumin and smoked paprika to taste.

1 LARGE SWEET POTATO (ABOUT 1 LB [455 G])

⅓ CUP [75 ML] TAHINI

⅓ CUP [75 ML] EXTRA-VIRGIN OLIVE OIL, PLUS MORE FOR DRIZZLING

ONE 15-OZ [425-G] CAN CHICKPEAS, DRAINED (LIQUID RESERVED)

1 LARGE GARLIC CLOVE, COARSELY CHOPPED

3 TBSP FRESH LEMON JUICE, OR MORE TO TASTE

1½ TSP KOSHER SALT, OR MORE TO TASTE

½ TSP SMOKED PAPRIKA
½ TSP GROUND CUMIN
CHOPPED FRESH CILANTRO FOR SERVING

1. Preheat the oven to 400°F [200°C]. Pierce the sweet potato in several places with the tip of a sharp knife and place on a baking sheet. Bake until completely tender, 45 to 60 minutes. Remove from the heat, carefully cut in half to facilitate cooling, and let cool to the touch.

2. When cool enough to handle, remove and discard the sweet potato skin. Combine the sweet potato flesh, tahini, $1/3$ cup [75 ml] olive oil, drained chickpeas, garlic, lemon juice, salt, paprika, and cumin in a food processor and process until a thick paste forms, scraping down the sides of the processor bowl as necessary. With the machine running, slowly pour in between $1/4$ cup [60 ml] and $1/3$ cup [75 ml] of the reserved chickpea liquid and continue processing until the mixture is smooth and creamy, 2 to 3 minutes. Transfer to a shallow bowl or plate, drizzle with olive oil, and sprinkle with cilantro. Store leftovers in an airtight container in the refrigerator for up to 1 week.

NEXT-LEVEL DIPPERS

Delicious dips and spreads deserve so much more than a plate of watery baby carrots to scoop them up. Here are some of my favorite crudités and crackers that will do them justice.

Sliced watermelon radishes

Sugar snap peas

Heirloom cherry tomatoes

Sliced jicama

Endive leaves

Fennel wedges

Purple cauliflower florets

Steamed asparagus

Steamed fingerling potatoes

Scottish oatcakes

Black sesame rice crisps

Root vegetable chips

Everything-Spice Rye Crackers (page 39)

Za'atar-Garlic Pita Chips (page 43)

Eggplant Carpaccio

SERVES 4 TO 6

Across Israel, particularly in upscale restaurants like Ezra Kedem's Arcadia, eggplant carpaccio—a charred eggplant that gets lightly smashed with a fork and paired with tahini, yogurt, chopped herbs, tomato, and lemon—has become a de rigueur appetizer. The name is actually a misnomer as traditional beef carpaccio is served raw, but it sounds fancy. More importantly, the mix of smoky, creamy, rich, and bright flavors epitomizes the region's magical touch with simple ingredients, and is truly irresistible.

Eggplant carpaccio is also wonderfully versatile. There are literally dozens of variations on the theme. So if you fancy parsley instead of mint, za'atar (page 128) instead of oregano, or silan (date honey) instead of bees' honey, swap away. If you keep kosher and want this dish to open a meat meal, omit the yogurt. And if you're serving a larger crowd, char up a few more eggplants and add a few extra dollops of all the toppings.

**2 MEDIUM EGGPLANTS (ABOUT 1 LB [455 G]),
GREEN TOPS TRIMMED BACK, WITH STEM LEFT INTACT**

1 RIPE LARGE PLUM TOMATO, DICED

¼ CUP [60 G] FULL-FAT PLAIN YOGURT

2 TBSP FRESH LEMON JUICE

2 TBSP TAHINI

2 TBSP MILD HONEY

2 TBSP CHOPPED FRESH OREGANO

2 TBSP CHOPPED FRESH MINT

FLAKY SEA SALT

1. Char the eggplants: Prick each eggplant in several places with a fork, then wrap tightly in two layers of aluminum foil. Place each eggplant directly on a grate of a gas stove-top. Turn the heat under the grates to medium and cook, rotating every few minutes with tongs, until the flesh is very tender, 15 to 20 minutes. Don't walk too far from the stove while the eggplants are cooking. Remove the eggplants from the heat, carefully unwrap them (the skin should be blistered and wrinkly), and place them in a colander to drain and let cool to the touch, about 20 minutes. Using a sharp knife, carefully scrape off the skin and discard.

2. Arrange the peeled eggplants on a small serving platter. Using a fork, gently smash the flesh to flatten it a bit. Scatter the tomato over the top and dollop spoonfuls of yogurt around the plate and on top of the eggplant. Drizzle with the lemon juice, tahini, and honey, then scatter with oregano, mint, and salt to taste. Serve warm or at room temperature.

Green Matbucha

SERVES 8

This North African tomato-pepper relish captures the
essence of summer. Made from tomatoes, peppers, and
sometimes eggplant, it gets cooked down with garlic
and chiles to create a silky relish that is popular throughout Middle Eastern cuisine, including in Israel. My version
blends a shock of vibrant green herbs and dried za'atar into
the classic recipe. Matbucha is often served as part of the
mezze course along with challah, crackers, or Za'atar-Garlic
Pita Chips (page 43), but also tastes delicious spooned over
eggs, chicken, or baked fish.

¼ CUP [60 ML] PLUS 2 TBSP EXTRA-VIRGIN OLIVE OIL

1 MEDIUM ONION, FINELY CHOPPED

**2 CUPS [160 G] PEELED CHOPPED EGGPLANT, CUT INTO
½-IN [12-MM] CUBES**

**1 MEDIUM GREEN BELL PEPPER, SEEDED AND CUT INTO
½-IN [12-MM] PIECES**

1 JALAPEÑO, SEEDED AND FINELY CHOPPED

1 TBSP SUGAR

KOSHER SALT AND FRESHLY GROUND BLACK PEPPER

6 GARLIC CLOVES, FINELY CHOPPED

2 TSP ZA'ATAR, PLUS MORE FOR SERVING

½ TSP ONION POWDER

½ TSP RED PEPPER FLAKES, OR MORE TO TASTE

ONE 15-OZ [425-G] CAN DICED TOMATOES

2 PACKED CUPS [50 G] FRESH BASIL LEAVES

1 PACKED CUP [25 G] FRESH MINT LEAVES

1. Heat ¼ cup [60 ml] of the olive oil in a large saucepan set over medium heat. Add the onion, eggplant, bell pepper, jalapeño, sugar, and a generous pinch of salt and cook, stirring occasionally, until the vegetables soften, about 15 minutes. Add the garlic, za'atar, onion powder, and red pepper flakes and cook, stirring, until fragrant, 1 to 2 minutes.

2. Stir in the tomatoes with their juice and bring to a simmer. Turn the heat to low and cook, partially covered and stirring often, until the mixture thickens and the vegetables grow very tender, about 10 minutes. Partway through cooking, mash the vegetables a bit with a potato masher or the back of a spoon.

3. Meanwhile, combine the basil, mint, another generous pinch of salt, and the remaining 2 tablespoons olive oil in a food processor and pulse until a pesto-like paste forms, scraping down the sides of the processor bowl as necessary.

4. Stir the herb mixture into the eggplant mixture and continue to cook until the matbucha thickens slightly, about 5 minutes. Remove from the heat and season with salt and black pepper to taste. Let cool to room temperature, then transfer to a serving bowl and sprinkle with more za'atar. Serve warm or at room temperature. Store, covered, in the refrigerator for up to 3 days.

Muhammara

SERVES 6

Muhammara is one of the crowning jewels of the Middle Eastern mezze spread. Originally from Aleppo, Syria, and popular throughout the region, it purées roasted red bell peppers with walnuts, pomegranate molasses, bread crumbs, and cumin into a textured spread with a flavor as vibrant as the dish's sunset color. Middle Eastern Jews serve muhammara as an appetizer with pita for swiping, or as part of the main meal, alongside fried eggplant slices or grilled meat.

Pomegranate molasses, which plays a starring role in muhammara, is made from pomegranate juice that gets boiled down into a tangy condensed syrup. It is possible to buy pomegranate molasses at Middle Eastern grocery stores and online (page 126). But if you need to go the DIY route, simply simmer about ½ cup [120 ml] of bottled 100-percent pomegranate juice in a saucepan set over medium heat, stirring often, until it reduces and coats the back of a spoon, 10 to 15 minutes. Any leftover molasses not needed for the dip tastes wonderful drizzled over baked fish, grain dishes, and cheese.

½ CUP [55 G] WALNUT HALVES

7 OZ [200 G] JAR ROASTED RED BELL PEPPERS, DRAINED WELL AND COARSELY CHOPPED

2 SCALLIONS, WHITE AND GREEN PARTS, COARSELY CHOPPED

⅓ CUP [40 G] UNSEASONED DRIED BREAD CRUMBS

1 SMALL GARLIC CLOVE, PEELED

1 TSP DRIED MINT, PLUS MORE FOR GARNISH
½ TSP RED PEPPER FLAKES, OR MORE TO TASTE
1 TSP GROUND CUMIN
2 TSP FRESH LEMON JUICE, OR MORE TO TASTE
1 TBSP POMEGRANATE MOLASSES
½ TSP KOSHER SALT, OR MORE TO TASTE
⅓ CUP [75 ML] EXTRA-VIRGIN OLIVE OIL, PLUS MORE FOR DRIZZLING
FRESH POMEGRANATE SEEDS FOR GARNISH

1. Place the walnuts in a small skillet and set over medium heat. Cook, shaking the pan occasionally, until fragrant and lightly browned, 5 to 7 minutes. Remove from the heat and transfer to a cutting board to cool. When cool enough to handle, coarsely chop.

2. Combine the walnuts, roasted peppers, scallions, bread crumbs, garlic, mint, red pepper flakes, cumin, lemon juice, pomegranate molasses, and salt in a food processor and pulse until a chunky paste forms, scraping down the sides of the processor bowl as necessary. With the machine running, drizzle in the olive oil and process until combined. Taste and add more salt, red pepper flakes, and lemon juice, if desired. Be careful not to go overboard as the flavors will continue to develop while the dish rests.

3. Transfer the muhammara to a wide serving bowl or plate and make a shallow well in the center with the back of a spoon. Sprinkle the pomegranate seeds and a little dried mint in the well, then drizzle a little more olive oil over the top. Serve immediately. Store leftovers in an airtight container in the refrigerator for up to 3 days.

Perfect Tzatziki

SERVES 6 TO 8

The winning combination of yogurt, chopped cucumbers, and garlic can be found throughout much of Turkey, Iran, Armenia, Lebanon, and Greece, among other places. Depending on where you are, it is either eaten as a dip, sauce, or salad, or thinned into a chilled soup. Sephardi Jews traditionally dip fried eggplant or pita into it or use it as a sauce for fish. Sometimes ground walnuts, dill, or rose petals are added, or the yogurt is replaced with tahini. Variations of the dish go by several names, including *cacik*, *tarator*, *khyar bi leban*, and perhaps the most widely known option, tzatziki.

Tzatziki is simple enough to make, but getting it just right takes a little finesse. I like to add a dollop of sour cream to the yogurt for added richness, and stir in a hint of bright lemon zest along with the minced garlic. I also grate the cucumbers instead of chopping them, which helps them blend into the sauce, and I squeeze the liquid out of the cucumbers to avoid the all-too-common pitfall of runny tzatziki. As a devotee to all creamy dressings—I am originally from the Midwest after all, where ranch dressing is king—I felt compelled to develop a perfect rendition of tzatziki. If I may say so, I think this version gets pretty close. Serve it with homemade pita chips (page 43) and sliced fresh vegetables for dipping.

1½ CUPS [300 G] FULL-FAT OR 2% GREEK YOGURT

½ CUP [100 G] SOUR CREAM

1 TBSP EXTRA-VIRGIN OLIVE OIL

¼ TSP GRATED LEMON ZEST

1 TBSP FRESH LEMON JUICE

1 TSP WHITE WINE VINEGAR

1 LARGE GARLIC CLOVE, MINCED OR PUSHED THROUGH A PRESS

2 TSP DRIED DILL

KOSHER SALT AND FRESHLY GROUND BLACK PEPPER

5 SMALL PERSIAN OR KIRBY CUCUMBERS, PEELED AND GRATED ON THE LARGE HOLES OF A BOX GRATER

1. In a medium bowl, stir together the yogurt, sour cream, olive oil, lemon zest, lemon juice, vinegar, garlic, dill, 1/2 tsp salt, and pepper to taste.

2. Place the grated cucumbers in the center of a dish towel and squeeze out as much liquid as possible. Fold the cucumbers into the yogurt mixture. Cover and refrigerate for at least 1 hour or overnight to let the flavors meld. Before serving, taste and add a little more salt if desired. Serve cold. Store leftovers, covered, in the refrigerator for up to 3 days.

Moroccan Orange and Black Olive Salad

SERVES 6

Moroccan cuisine brilliantly uses oranges as the base
for many different sweet-savory salads, but oranges and
olives are perhaps the most iconic duo. While it may
sound unusual, the combination of sweet citrus and briny,
velvet-textured, oil-cured black olives (page 126) is
nothing short of magical.

In Moroccan Jewish homes, this salad is often served as
part of the sprawling mezze course—a refreshing opener
to Shabbat dinner. A drizzle of oil (traditionally Moroccan
argan oil) and a sprinkle of salt is all that's needed to pull
the flavors together. But why not gild the lily with a little
smoky spice, bright lime juice, and a drizzle of honey for
extra sweetness?

¼ CUP [60 ML] EXTRA-VIRGIN OLIVE OIL

2 TBSP FRESH LIME JUICE

1 TBSP HONEY

**1 SMALL GARLIC CLOVE, MINCED OR
PUSHED THROUGH A PRESS**

½ TSP GROUND CUMIN

¼ TSP SMOKED PAPRIKA

⅛ TSP RED PEPPER FLAKES

½ TSP KOSHER SALT

6 NAVEL ORANGES

**1 CUP [160 G] OIL-CURED BLACK OLIVES, PITTED AND
COARSELY CHOPPED**

CHOPPED FRESH FLAT-LEAF PARSLEY FOR SERVING

1. In a small bowl, whisk together the olive oil, lime juice, honey, garlic, cumin, paprika, red pepper flakes, and salt. Set aside.

2. Using a sharp serrated knife, slice off the ends of each orange. Stand one orange upright on one of its flat ends. Starting at the top, cut away a section of the peel, following the curve of the fruit to the bottom and taking care to remove all the white pith. Continue in this manner around the fruit, until all the peel is gone. Lay the orange on its rounded side and cut into 1/2-in [12-mm] wheels. Repeat with the remaining oranges.

3. Arrange the orange slices on a platter. Scatter the olives and parsley over the top and drizzle evenly with the dressing. Serve immediately.

Everything–Spice Rye Crackers

SERVES 6

The everything bagel—which comes topped with a mix of poppy and sesame seeds, dehydrated garlic and onion, and salt—is a relatively recent invention. According to Jewish baking legend, back in the 1980s, a genius baker came up with the idea while sweeping excess seeds out of his oven after closing up his shop for the night. The flavor mash-up caught on quickly and became a perennial favorite. More recently, "everything" spice has begun to crop up in other dishes, from fried chicken to scones. Here, I sprinkle the addictive topping onto a simple dough (honest!) to make snappy homemade rye crackers. I now make these crisps all the time and use them while snacking on Chopped Egg and Caramelized Onion Spread (page 12), Vegetarian Chopped Liver with Shallots (page 15), and many other savory dips.

Powdered ground garlic and onion are too concentrated for this recipe and will overwhelm the subtle rye flavor, so be sure to use dehydrated flakes instead. The recipe makes more of the spice mix than you need for the crackers. Store the extra in a small bowl on your kitchen counter and sprinkle it onto scrambled eggs, popcorn, pasta, roasted veggies, fresh salads, or any other dish that could use an extra kick.

1 TBSP POPPY SEEDS

1 TBSP SESAME SEEDS

1 TBSP DEHYDRATED GARLIC FLAKES

1 TBSP DEHYDRATED ONION FLAKES

2 TSP KOSHER SALT

CRACKERS

1¼ CUPS [155 G] ALL-PURPOSE FLOUR

1 CUP [115 G] RYE FLOUR

1 TSP KOSHER SALT

½ TSP BAKING POWDER

½ CUP PLUS 2 TBSP [150 ML] COW'S MILK OR ALMOND MILK

**¼ CUP [60 ML] EXTRA-VIRGIN OLIVE OIL,
PLUS MORE FOR BRUSHING**

1. To make the spice mix: Stir together the poppy seeds, sesame seeds, garlic flakes, onion flakes, and salt in a small bowl. Set aside.

2. To make the crackers: Preheat the oven to 350°F [180°C] and line 2 large rimmed baking sheets with parchment paper. In a large bowl, whisk together the all-purpose flour, rye flour, salt, and baking powder. Make a well in the center of the dry ingredients and pour in the milk and olive oil. Stir with a wooden spoon until the mixture begins to come together.

40

3. Turn the dough onto a lightly floured surface and knead it a couple of times with your hands to bring it together. Use a rolling pin to roll the dough as thinly as possible into a large rectangle, less than 1/8 in [4 mm] thick. Trim any ragged edges with a sharp knife. Use a fork to prick the dough all over, then brush a thin, even layer of olive oil over the surface. Sprinkle the dough with the everything spice mixture (you won't use all of it).

4. Using a sharp knife or pizza cutter, cut the crackers into small squares or rectangles. There's no need to be specific with measuring here—just cut them into whatever size you like. Transfer the crackers to the prepared baking sheets, spacing them about 1/2 in [12 mm] apart.

5. Bake, rotating the baking sheets halfway through cooking, until the crackers are firm and golden brown around the edges, 17 to 20 minutes. Remove from the oven and transfer the baking sheets to cooling racks; let cool completely before serving. Store the crackers in an airtight container at room temperature for up to 1 week.

Za'atar–Garlic Pita Chips

SERVES 6

Homemade pita chips are delicious, arguably even more so than their store-bought counterparts. They are also simple to make. A little olive oil, a sprinkle of salt and pepper, and a few minutes in the oven are all that's necessary to transform plain rounds of pita into a delightful snack or dip accompaniment. This version dresses up the crisps with garlic-infused oil and a hit of the lemony, herbal Middle Eastern spice mixture, za'atar (page 128). They are special enough to serve as party hors d'oeuvres and easy enough to bake up for a weeknight snack. If you are starting with extra-fluffy pita, they may take a few extra minutes to bake.

⅓ CUP [75 ML] EXTRA-VIRGIN OLIVE OIL
3 GARLIC CLOVES, MINCED OR PUSHED THROUGH A PRESS
3 TBSP ZA'ATAR
1 TSP ONION POWDER
4 LARGE WHITE OR WHOLE-WHEAT PITAS
KOSHER SALT AND FRESHLY GROUND BLACK PEPPER

1. Preheat the oven to 375°F [190°C]. Heat the oil in a small saucepan set over low heat. Add the garlic and cook, stirring, until fragrant and sizzling, about 1 minute. Remove from the heat and let sit 10 minutes to infuse the oil with the garlic. Whisk in the za'atar and onion powder and set aside.

2. Slice each round of pita into 8 equal wedges. Brush both sides of each wedge lightly with the za'atar-garlic oil and arrange them in a single layer on two large rimmed baking sheets. Sprinkle evenly with the salt and pepper to taste.

3. Bake, rotating the baking sheets and flipping the pita wedges with tongs halfway through cooking, until the pita is crisp and golden brown, 10 to 15 minutes. Remove from the oven and transfer baking sheets to cooling racks to let chips cool completely. Serve at room temperature. Store leftovers in an airtight container for up to 3 days. Reheat the pita chips in a 350°F [180°C] oven for about 4 minutes.

Borscht Crostini

SERVES 6

Whether served hot or cold, brimming with meat or completely vegetarian, the beet soup known as borscht has
become a staple of the Ashkenazi Jewish repertoire. Perhaps that is because, amidst a sea of brown, heavy dishes—
potato kugel, challah, cholent, latkes, and so on—borscht's
ruby color and tangy-sweet flavor offers a bright counter-
point. I love to make borscht, but I do not fancy the cold
version that is popular during the warm summer months.
Instead, I transfer all the soup's building blocks—roasted
beets and carrots, pickled onions, fresh dill and garlic,
and crème fraîche (aka fancy sour cream)—from the soup
bowl to a piece of crunchy toast. The resulting crostini are
visually stunning (red beets! springy chopped herbs!) and
versatile enough to serve as party fare or be the center
of a summertime snack or meal. Each component can be
prepped in advance and assembled just before serving.

**3 MEDIUM BEETS, PEELED, HALVED, AND CUT INTO
½-IN [12-MM] CHUNKS**

**4 MEDIUM CARROTS, PEELED, HALVED LENGTHWISE,
AND CUT INTO 2-IN [5-CM] LENGTHS**

3 TBSP RED WINE VINEGAR

2 TBSP EXTRA-VIRGIN OLIVE OIL, PLUS MORE FOR BRUSHING

KOSHER SALT AND FRESHLY GROUND BLACK PEPPER

¼ CUP [60 ML] FRESH LIME JUICE

2 TBSP SUGAR

**1 SMALL RED ONION, QUARTERED THROUGH THE ROOT
AND SLICED AS THINLY AS POSSIBLE**

¾ CUP [35 G] CHOPPED FRESH DILL

ZEST OF 1 LEMON

1 LARGE GARLIC CLOVE, COARSELY CHOPPED

12 SMALL, ½-INCH- [12-MM-] THICK SLICES OF SOURDOUGH OR RYE BREAD

ONE 8-OZ [225-G] CONTAINER CRÈME FRAÎCHE OR SOUR CREAM

1. Preheat the oven to 450°F [230°C] and line a large rimmed baking sheet with aluminum foil. Put the beets, carrots, 2 Tbsp red wine vinegar, 2 Tbsp olive oil, ½ tsp salt, and a generous amount of pepper on the baking sheet and stir to coat. Bake, tossing once with tongs, until the vegetables are tender, 25 to 35 minutes. Remove from the heat and let cool to the touch.

2. Meanwhile, in a medium bowl, whisk together the remaining 1 Tbsp of red wine vinegar, the lime juice, sugar, and a pinch of salt. Add the onion slices and toss to coat. Let sit for 15 to 20 minutes, stirring once or twice, to soften and lightly pickle the onion. (Or cover and let sit in the refrigerator for up to 1 day.)

3. Place the dill, lemon zest, and garlic in a single mound on a cutting board and chop until the garlic is minced and the ingredients are well combined.

4. Turn the oven to 400°F [200°C]. Brush one side of the bread slices with olive oil, sprinkle with salt, and arrange on two large baking sheets. Bake until crisp and golden, 8 to 10 minutes. Remove from the oven and let cool slightly.

5. To assemble the crostini: Spread each bread slice with about 1 Tbsp of crème fraîche and top with a few pieces of beet and carrot and some pickled onion slices. Sprinkle with the dill mixture and more black pepper. Serve immediately.

Smoked Trout Canapés

Smoked trout may not be as well known within Jewish cuisine as lox or cured herring, but it makes a worthy addition to any fish plate. First brined and then hot-smoked over wood, trout fillets come out of the smoker tender and delicately flavored. These canapés pair the smoked trout (page 127) with a bright and creamy spread and come together in about 10 minutes, making them a low-stress, high-impact starter or appetizer. I like to lay out a tray of them at a Hanukkah party to give guests something substantial to nibble on while the latkes are frying.

6 OZ [170 G] CREAM CHEESE, AT ROOM TEMPERATURE
1 TBSP BRINE-PACKED CAPERS, DRAINED
2 TSP FRESH LEMON JUICE
2 SCALLIONS, WHITE AND GREEN PARTS, THINLY SLICED
KOSHER SALT AND FRESHLY GROUND BLACK PEPPER
12 SLICES PUMPERNICKEL BREAD, ABOUT 3-IN [7.5-CM] SQUARE
8 OZ [225 G] SMOKED TROUT, BONES REMOVED AND FLAKED
SNIPPED FRESH CHIVES FOR SERVING

1. Combine the cream cheese, capers, lemon juice, scallions, and a pinch of salt in a food processor and process until smooth.

2. Spread a rounded tablespoon of the cream cheese mixture onto each piece of bread. Layer a few flakes of trout on top and sprinkle with chives and black pepper to taste. Serve immediately.

Pickled Cherry Tomatoes

SERVES 8

At the turn of the twentieth century, New York's Lower
East Side was awash in pickles. There, scores of Jewish
pushcart merchants sold pickled cucumbers, yes, but also
whole pickled cabbages, pickled watermelons, mushrooms,
eggplants, beets, string beans, and tomatoes. Several
decades later in Brooklyn, food writer and historian Arthur
Schwartz remembers enjoying pickled tomatoes with his
family. "At my mother's table, whenever we ate a big Jewish
meal . . . there was always a pretty plate of sours in the middle," he writes in *Arthur Schwartz's Jewish Home Cooking:
Yiddish Recipes Revisited.* "They were colorful decor, and
to my mother a necessary reminder, a vestige, of where
we came from."

Back then, Jewish home cooks typically pickled unripe
green tomatoes. But I love pickling ruby-hued cherry tomatoes fresh from the farmers' market. After a few days in the
refrigerator, they begin to shrivel just a bit while soaking
in all that delicious pickled flavor. Biting into one releases
a pop of brine and an unbeatable rush of summer. These
refrigerator-pickled cherry tomatoes are a wonderful addition to salads and a great snack on their own. I also love
adding them to cheese plates (page 58) or serving them
as part of the mezze selection at Shabbat dinner. If you
are planning to serve these for a specific dinner or party,
make them three or four days in advance so the flavor
has time to develop.

½ CUP [120 ML] APPLE CIDER VINEGAR
¼ CUP [60 ML] WHITE WINE VINEGAR
1 CUP [240 ML] WATER
1 TBSP KOSHER SALT
2 TSP SUGAR
3 CUPS [480 G] CHERRY OR GRAPE TOMATOES
4 GARLIC CLOVES, THINLY SLICED
¼ PACKED CUP [15G] FRESH DILL (STEMS OKAY)
1 SPRIG ROSEMARY
2 TSP BLACK PEPPERCORNS

1. Combine the apple cider vinegar, white wine vinegar, water, salt, and sugar in a small saucepan and set over medium-high heat. Bring to a boil, stirring to dissolve the sugar and salt. Remove from the heat and let cool for 15 to 20 minutes.

2. Use the tip of a very sharp knife to lightly pierce each tomato in 2 or 3 places. Pack the tomatoes into a clean, dry 1-qt [1-L] glass jar along with the garlic, dill, rosemary, and peppercorns. Pour the vinegar mixture over the top to cover the tomatoes. Cover the jar with a dish towel and let stand until the brine cools completely, at least 2 hours. Cover the jar with a lid and refrigerate for up to 2 weeks. The flavor will continue to develop in the refrigerator. Serve cold.

Beet–Pickled Turnips

SERVES 6 TO 8

Turnips are the cucumbers of the Middle Eastern pickle
canon. The term *turshi* refers to any type of pickle, but the
sharp, bulbous root is the most commonly brined vegetable
by far. Turnips pickled with beets (added for sweetness and
their stunning red color) are a mainstay of the Middle Eastern Shabbat dinner mezze spread. This version is incredibly simple to make and delivers crunchy, bright pickles that
are delicious straight out of the jar or layered on a sandwich. They also add color to a pickles and olives plate.

2 CUPS [480 ML] WATER

2 TBSP KOSHER SALT

¼ CUP [60 ML] APPLE CIDER VINEGAR

**1 LB [455 G] WHITE TURNIPS, PEELED, QUARTERED, AND CUT INTO
¼-IN [6-MM] SLICES**

**1 SMALL BEET, PEELED, QUARTERED, AND CUT INTO
¼-IN [6-MM] SLICES**

4 GARLIC CLOVES, PEELED AND SMASHED

¼ TSP RED PEPPER FLAKES

1 TSP EXTRA-VIRGIN OLIVE OIL

1. Combine the water, salt, and vinegar in a small saucepan
and set over medium-high heat. Bring to a boil, stirring to
dissolve the salt, then remove from the heat.

2. Pack the turnips, beet, garlic, and red pepper flakes into a clean, dry 1-qt [1-L] glass jar. Pour as much brine as possible over the vegetables to cover them (you may not need all the brine). Cover the jar with a dish towel and let stand until the brine cools completely, at least 2 hours. Drizzle the olive oil over the top, cover the jar with a lid, and let sit for 3 to 5 days at room temperature, depending on how strong-flavored and tender you like your pickles. (If you taste the turnips while they are pickling, be sure to use a clean spoon to remove them from the jar, not your fingers!)

Cover and refrigerate for up to 3 weeks. Serve cold.

A JEWISH
CHEESE PLATE

There is something so beguiling about a well-curated cheese plate offset by an array of colorful fruits, preserves, olives, and other treats. So when I started to dream up a collection of dishes for a Jewish appetizer book, a Jewish cheese plate felt like a must.

From salty grilled halloumi to tangy labneh, there are some real delights within the global Jewish cheese tradition that are worth showcasing. Meanwhile, the growing boutique cheese movement going on in Israel right now, as well as a handful of artisanal kosher cheese makers in the United States—5 Spoke Creamery in New York state, Narragansett Creamery in Rhode Island, and Redwood Hill Farm & Creamery in California (see page 125 for sources)—have begun to expand the landscape in delicious ways.

The cheeses below include some of my favorites used in Jewish cuisine. When putting together a Jewishly inspired cheese plate for a party or low-key get-together, you can either stick strictly to the list, or use them to augment more standard cheese plate favorites like crumbly aged Cheddar, a gooey triple crème, and toffee-colored Gouda. As with all cheese plates, try to include a range of textures from soft and spreadable to firm and crumbly, with flavors from mild to strong.

I have also included some suggested accompaniments—the pickles, jams, and crackers that will add Jewish flair to your edible composition. Go for lots of color and sweet-savory contrast, or keep it simple with one or two carefully chosen pairings. Either way, your guests are bound to come flocking.

THE CHEESES

Braided Cheese

This Middle Eastern cheese is made from strips of mozzarella-like cheese that are twisted into a thick braid. It often comes flavored with pungent, black nigella seeds.

Farmer Cheese

In Jewish cooking, this mild, unripened curd cheese is typically used as the filling for Eastern European dishes like blintzes. But it works great as part of a cheese plate too. Serve it in a small bowl with a cocktail knife for spreading. Amp up the flavor by stirring in a little grated orange zest and honey.

Feta

While often crumbled into a salad, larger blocks of sheep's milk feta are wonderful on a cheese plate. Feta is a common addition to *sabzi khordan*, a free-form platter of fresh herbs, cheese, and toasted nuts that is typically served at the beginning of a Persian meal. Dress up the feta by toasting ground spices like cumin and coriander in a skillet, mixing the spices with olive oil, and drizzling it over the cheese.

Fresh Goat Cheese

This soft, spreadable fresh cheese—also called chèvre—has a mildly sharp flavor. Enhance a plain log of goat cheese by spreading a layer of za'atar, paprika, or black and white sesame seeds on a plate, and gently pressing the cheese into the herb mix or seeds, turning to make sure it's coated on all sides.

Halloumi

Hailing from Greek and Turkish cuisine, and now enjoyed throughout Israel, halloumi is an unripened brined cheese made from a mix of goat's and sheep's milk. Its salty, slightly gamy flavor really shines when it is grilled. To prepare it for your cheese plate (or any other dish), preheat a gas or charcoal grill or set a grill pan over medium heat. Cut the halloumi into 1/2-in [12 mm] slices. Brush each side with a little olive oil and grill, turning once, until grill marks form and the cheese warms through, 2 to 4 minutes per side.

Kashkaval

Popular in Bulgaria, Romania, and parts of the Middle East, this semihard cheese, made from either cow's or sheep's milk, is delicately flavored.

Labneh

This Middle Eastern strained yogurt is thick and creamy like Greek yogurt and has a pleasantly sour taste. To include it on a cheese plate, place a hearty dollop in a small bowl and top it with a sprinkle of za'atar and a drizzle of olive oil.

EVERYTHING ELSE

Sour cherries in syrup (drained)

Prune or apricot preserves

Dried or fresh figs or dates

Pomegranate seeds

Fresh apple or pear slices

Slivers of halvah

Honey or silan (date honey)

Quartered radishes

Fresh basil, flat-leaf parsley, or mint leaves

Caramelized onions

Cornichons or pickle spears

Olives

Pickled Cherry Tomatoes (page 52)

Beet-Pickled Turnips (page 55)

Everything-Spice Rye Crackers (page 39)

Za'atar-Garlic Pita Chips (page 43)

Sourdough toasts

Brown bread

CHAPTER 2

COOKED, FRIED, BAKED

Whet guests' appetites with this collection of bite-size cooked and fried dishes, including Sephardi meatballs, shiitake-studded falafel, and English-style fried gefilte fish. This section is rounded out with a few globally inspired, snackable baked goods, from mushroom-filled Russian piroshki to the coiled Sephardi pastries known as *bulemas*.

Barley-Stuffed Mushrooms

SERVES 6 TO 8

Mushrooms and barley were fixtures of the Eastern European Jewish kitchen, most notably paired in a nourishing bowl of mushroom barley soup. This appetizer also features the iconic duo, but showcases them a little differently. Here, mushroom caps are stuffed with tender barley that has been dressed up with Parmesan, fresh herbs, and a splash of white wine and served as two-bite hors d'oeuvres. The charming little caps would be at home as a first course on the Sukkot table, since the harvest holiday's menu tends to feature stuffed foods. But I like to serve them as party fare, paired with a glass of white wine.

½ CUP [100 G] PEARL BARLEY

KOSHER SALT AND FRESHLY GROUND BLACK PEPPER

24 LARGE CREMINI OR WHITE MUSHROOMS, CLEANED WITH A PAPER TOWEL

2 TBSP UNSALTED BUTTER, PLUS MORE FOR GREASING THE BAKING SHEET

1 SMALL SHALLOT, FINELY CHOPPED

3 GARLIC CLOVES, MINCED OR PUSHED THROUGH A PRESS

½ CUP [120 ML] DRY WHITE WINE

1 CUP [30 G] FINELY GRATED PARMESAN CHEESE

½ CUP [25 G] FINELY CHOPPED FRESH FLAT-LEAF PARSLEY

1 TBSP FINELY CHOPPED FRESH THYME

EXTRA-VIRGIN OLIVE OIL FOR DRIZZLING

1. Fill a medium pot with 5 cups [1.2 L] of water and set over high heat. When the water boils, stir in the barley and a large pinch of salt, then turn the heat to medium. Cook, stirring occasionally, until the barley is tender but still chewy, 35 to 40 minutes. Drain and transfer to a large bowl; set aside to cool.

2. Preheat the oven to 375°F [190°C] and grease a large rimmed baking sheet. Remove the stems from the mushrooms and finely chop them; reserve the caps. Melt the 2 Tbsp butter in a medium skillet set over medium-high heat. Add the chopped mushroom stems, the shallot, and garlic, season with salt, and cook, stirring occasionally, until the mushrooms are soft and most of their liquid evaporates, 6 to 8 minutes. Add 1/4 cup [60 ml] of the wine and cook until it evaporates, about 3 minutes. Remove the skillet from heat and set aside to cool slightly.

3. Stir the Parmesan, parsley, thyme, and cooked mushroom mixture into the cooled barley. Season with salt and pepper to taste. Use a spoon and your hands to stuff the mushroom caps with the filling, packing each one tightly and mounding some on top.

4. Arrange the filled mushroom caps in a single layer on the prepared baking sheet. Pour the remaining 1/4 cup [60 ml] wine around the mushrooms and drizzle a little olive oil over the tops. Bake until golden brown, about 30 minutes. Serve warm. Store leftovers, covered, in the refrigerator for up to 3 days. Reheat in an oven or toaster oven at 350°F [180°C] until warmed through, 10 to 15 minutes.

Persian Zucchini and Herb Frittata

SERVES 8

Fresh herbs are paramount in Persian cooking, and *kukus*—the Middle Eastern answer to frittatas—are a wonderful place to showcase them. This version pairs softened matchsticks of zucchini with briny feta and verdant heaps of fresh parsley, dill, and oregano. Because it tastes equally good warm or at room temperature, a kuku is an incredibly versatile dish. Jews traditionally served it as part of the mezze course or as a side dish on Shabbat, but it would hardly be out of place at Sunday brunch. Cut into small squares and topped with a little yogurt or crème fraîche, it also doubles as a delightful party appetizer. And I've been known to sneak a wedge straight from the refrigerator when a mid-afternoon hunger pang strikes. Sub in matzo meal for the flour on Passover, or use a gluten-free all-purpose flour blend to make this dish effortlessly gluten-free.

⅓ CUP [75 ML] VEGETABLE OIL, PLUS MORE FOR BRUSHING

2 MEDIUM ONIONS, HALVED THROUGH THE ROOT AND THINLY SLICED

KOSHER SALT AND FRESHLY GROUND BLACK PEPPER

2 SMALL ZUCCHINI, CUT INTO 1-IN- [2.5-CM-] LONG MATCHSTICKS

7 EGGS

2 TBSP ALL-PURPOSE FLOUR

1 TSP BAKING POWDER

½ CUP [25 G] CHOPPED FRESH FLAT-LEAF PARSLEY

½ CUP [25 G] CHOPPED FRESH DILL

2 TBSP CHOPPED FRESH OREGANO

2 GARLIC CLOVES, MINCED OR PUSHED THROUGH A PRESS

1 TSP GROUND TURMERIC

1 TSP ONION POWDER

¼ TSP RED PEPPER FLAKES

1½ CUPS [150 G] CRUMBLED FETA

1. Preheat the oven to 375°F [190°C] and brush a 9-in [23-cm] springform or regular cake pan with oil. Use scissors to cut out a circle of parchment paper for the bottom of the pan and to cut a long strip to wrap around the sides. Line the bottom and sides of the pan with the parchment, then brush the parchment with oil.

2. Heat the ⅓ cup [75 ml] oil in a large sauté pan set over medium heat. Add the onions, season with a little salt, and cook, stirring occasionally, until softened and lightly browned, 8 to 10 minutes. Add the zucchini and continue to cook, stirring occasionally, until the zucchini softens and browns in spots, 10 to 12 minutes. Set aside to cool slightly.

3. In a large bowl, whisk together the eggs, flour, baking powder, parsley, dill, oregano, garlic, turmeric, onion powder, red pepper flakes, 3/4 tsp salt, and a generous amount of pepper. Fold in the zucchini mixture and feta. Pour into the prepared pan and bake until golden brown and cooked through, 30 to 40 minutes. Set aside to cool for 15 minutes. Gently remove from the pan and cut into wedges or squares. Serve warm or at room temperature. Store leftovers, covered, in the refrigerator for up to 2 days.

Fried Artichoke Hearts

SERVES 8

Rome's Jewish community stretches back to the second century BCE and has a cuisine all of its own. The most famous dish, *carciofi alla giudia*, or Jewish-style artichokes, bathes the lovely thistles in hot olive oil until they transform into crispy flowers. Salt-kissed fried artichokes are still served as an appetizer in Rome, particularly in the restaurants that dot the historic, and now very fashionable, Jewish ghetto neighborhood.

Jewish-style fried artichokes are seriously delicious. They are also a serious chore to prepare as each globe must be painstakingly trimmed of its thorny outer layers (only the tender inside part is used), relieved of its choke, and steamed before the frying begins. So instead, I offer a hacked version that begins with brined artichoke hearts that, like with *fritto misto* (another beloved dish with Roman Jewish roots), get battered and fried. While I wouldn't claim this take on fried artichokes to be just like *carciofi alla giudia*, they still make a crunchy and briny meal starter—without the fuss and overwhelming heap of kitchen scraps.

½ CUP [65 G] ALL-PURPOSE FLOUR

4 EGGS, LIGHTLY BEATEN

2 CUPS [120 G] UNSEASONED PANKO BREAD CRUMBS

**TWO 14-OZ [400-G] CANS QUARTERED ARTICHOKE HEARTS,
DRAINED AND PATTED DRY WITH PAPER TOWELS**

VEGETABLE OIL FOR FRYING

KOSHER SALT

LEMON WEDGES FOR SERVING

1. Line a large plate with a couple of layers of paper towels. Put the flour in a wide, shallow bowl, the eggs in a second bowl, and the bread crumbs in a third bowl. Dredge the artichoke hearts in the flour, shaking off excess. Dip in the egg, then dredge in the bread crumbs. Place on a separate plate while the oil heats.

2. Fill a large saucepan with $1/2$ in [12 mm] of oil and heat over medium heat until shimmering. Working in batches of 7 or 8, fry the artichokes until crisp and golden brown, turning once with tongs, 6 to 7 minutes per batch. Adjust the heat if the artichokes are browning too quickly and add more oil, if necessary. Use tongs or a slotted spoon to transfer the fried artichokes to the paper towel-lined plate and let drain. Sprinkle with salt and serve immediately, with lemon wedges on the side for squeezing.

Shiitake and Scallion Falafel

SERVES 8

Falafel is Middle Eastern snack food at its best. The vegan- and gluten-free-friendly chickpea croquettes (or often fava bean outside of Israel) check all the pleasure center boxes: crispy, tender, and savory. Falafel is Arab in origin, but has been widely adopted across Israel as a nationally beloved street food, where it is put into a split pita along with fresh and roasted vegetables, tahini, pickles, hummus, and sometimes french fries, to make a glorious sandwich.

In the spirit of improving upon perfection, I added sautéed shiitake mushrooms and scallions to a traditional chickpea falafel batter. The result is both subtle and profound, an extra dose of umami encapsulated in a delightfully crunchy package. Spear them with a toothpick and serve them as a vegetarian alternative to Albóndigas (page 80). Or eat them straight, dipped in mayo or hummus, or drizzled with an herby vinaigrette. For best results—especially if you are new to deep-frying—I suggest using a deep-fry thermometer, which is inexpensive and will ensure your oil is at just the right temperature before dropping the falafel balls into the pot. Also, do not substitute canned chickpeas; they are already cooked and their texture is too mushy for this recipe.

1 CUP [195 G] DRIED CHICKPEAS

2 TBSP EXTRA-VIRGIN OLIVE OIL

1 LB [455 G] SHIITAKE MUSHROOMS, CLEANED WITH A PAPER TOWEL, STEMMED, AND VERY FINELY CHOPPED

KOSHER SALT

2 SCALLIONS, WHITE AND GREEN PARTS, FINELY CHOPPED

1 TBSP HARISSA PASTE (PAGE 126)

½ SMALL ONION, COARSELY CHOPPED

4 GARLIC CLOVES, PEELED

½ CUP [25 G] CHOPPED FRESH FLAT-LEAF PARSLEY

3 TBSP CHICKPEA FLOUR (PAGE 125) OR ALL-PURPOSE FLOUR

2 TSP GROUND CUMIN

1 TSP GROUND CORIANDER

VEGETABLE OIL FOR FRYING

1. Place the chickpeas in a large bowl and cover with cold water by at least 2 in [5 cm]. Cover the bowl with a dish towel and let the chickpeas soak overnight at room temperature. Drain, rinse, then drain well again.

2. Heat the olive oil in a large skillet set over medium heat. Add the mushrooms and a generous pinch of salt and cook, stirring often, until the mushrooms are soft and most of their liquid evaporates, 8 to 10 minutes. Add the scallions and cook until just wilted, 1 to 2 minutes. Remove from the heat and stir in the harissa. Set aside and let cool to the touch.

3. Combine the soaked, uncooked chickpeas, the onion, garlic, parsley, chickpea flour, cumin, coriander, and 1½ tsp kosher salt in a food processor, and pulse until a textured paste forms, scraping down the sides of the processor bowl as necessary. If you squeeze a bit of the mixture in the palm of your hand, it should stick together. Stir in the mushroom mixture.

4. Line a large plate with a few layers of paper towels. Fill a deep pot with 1½ in [4 cm] of oil and heat over medium heat until the oil reaches 375°F [190°C] on a deep-fry thermometer. Meanwhile, scoop out a heaping tablespoon of the falafel mixture and use the palms of your hands and fingers to gently squeeze and roll it into a 1-in [2.5-cm] ball. The falafel batter might seem delicate at this point, but the ball will come together while frying. Set it on a baking sheet and continue forming balls with the remaining batter.

5. Working in batches of 5 or 6, carefully drop the falafel balls into the hot oil and fry until deep golden brown, 4 to 6 minutes per batch. Use a slotted spoon to transfer to the falafel to the prepared plate and let drain. Serve hot or warm. Store leftovers, covered, in the refrigerator for up to 5 days, or cover tightly in plastic wrap and store in the freezer for up to 3 months. Reheat in an oven or toaster oven at 350°F [180°C] until warmed through, 10 to 15 minutes.

ROUNDING OUT YOUR APPETIZER SPREAD

When planning a dinner or party, it is crucial to strike a balance between preparing beautiful, delicious food that your guests will appreciate and not burning out from all of the prep work. Appetizers do make the first impression, but that does not mean that everything has to be homemade. Keep it simple by choosing one (or two or three) appetizers to make from scratch and feature those at the center of your table. Then round out the selection with a few store-bought treats that require minimal preparation. Here are a few of my favorite premade or minimal-prep appetizers.

Fig jam spread on crackers

Caviar served with crackers and sour cream

Good-quality olives

Jarred roasted red peppers, drained

Jarred artichoke hearts, drained

Frozen bourekas, filled phyllo cigars, or spanakopita

Stuffed grape leaves

Roasted nuts such as Marcona almonds or pistachios

Miniature frozen latkes with store-bought applesauce or chutney

Albóndigas

In Brooklyn, husband and wife chefs Alex Raij and Eder Montero run La Vara, a small plates Spanish restaurant featuring the Jewish and Moorish flavors of pre-Inquisition Spain. Sound like a mouthful? It is—and a delicious one. In practice, that means the menu highlights the ingredients (like eggplants, chickpeas, artichokes, and almonds) and techniques (braising, deep-frying, and stewing) that evoke Medieval Spain, when Jewish and Muslim communities lived and cooked side by side.

Albóndigas, meatballs flavored with copious spices and fresh herbs, are a perfect example of how this ancient cuisine can taste right at home on the contemporary table. La Vara's albóndigas are made from lamb, but I prefer beef, which has a milder flavor that lets the spices and herbs shine. I also like to add finely chopped pine nuts along with the bread crumbs for extra savory flavor and crunch. These petite meatballs make perfect party appetizer fare. Arrange them on a platter with toothpicks stuck through the middle and a bowl of tahini dressed up with mint, lemon, and minced garlic for dipping.

2 LB [910 G] GROUND BEEF

1¼ TSP KOSHER SALT

1 TBSP GROUND CUMIN

1½ TSP GROUND CORIANDER

½ TSP GROUND CINNAMON

¼ TSP SMOKED PAPRIKA

¼ TSP CAYENNE PEPPER, OR MORE TO TASTE

2 TSP HARISSA PASTE (PAGE 126)

½ CUP [25 G] FINELY CHOPPED FRESH FLAT-LEAF PARSLEY

½ CUP [25 G] FINELY CHOPPED FRESH MINT

1 SMALL ONION, GRATED

3 GARLIC CLOVES, MINCED OR PUSHED THROUGH A PRESS

2 EGGS, LIGHTLY BEATEN

½ CUP [30 G] UNSEASONED PANKO BREAD CRUMBS
OR MATZO MEAL

¼ CUP [40 G] PINE NUTS, FINELY CHOPPED

2 TBSP VEGETABLE OIL, OR MORE AS NEEDED

1. Combine the beef, salt, cumin, coriander, cinnamon, paprika, cayenne, harissa, parsley, mint, onion, garlic, eggs, bread crumbs, and pine nuts in a large bowl. Using your hands, mix everything together until well combined.

2. Scoop out a heaping tablespoon of the beef mixture and, using the palms of your hands, roll it into a ball. Set it on a baking sheet and continue forming balls with the remaining beef mixture.

3. Heat the vegetable oil in a large skillet over medium heat. Working in batches of 7 or 8, add the meatballs and cook, turning with tongs, until cooked through and browned all over, 7 to 10 minutes. If the pan begins to look dry, add a little more oil. Serve hot. Store leftovers, covered, in the refrigerator for up to 3 days, or wrapped tightly in plastic wrap in the freezer for up to 3 months. Reheat in an oven or toaster oven at 350°F [180°C] until warmed through, 10 to 15 minutes.

Fried Gefilte Fish

SERVES 8 TO 10

Gefilte fish is one of the most iconic Ashkenazi Jewish appetizers, typically served at the beginning of Passover, Rosh Hashanah, and other Jewish holiday meals. It typically comes poached in fish broth and is served cold. Some people love it, but it is an acquired taste, to be sure. Jews in the United Kingdom have a delicious little secret: Instead of poaching their gefilte fish, they fry it. British Jews can also be found at the roots of fish and chips because it was the Portuguese Jews who were living in London's East End that introduced fried fish to the country in the seventeenth century. Fried gefilte is really just the next logical step.

Many fried gefilte fish recipes follow a basic latke format, using ground whitefish in place of shredded potatoes and swapping the flour with matzo meal. I like to add a bit of salmon to the mix and throw a sautéed onion into the batter (instead of grated fresh onion) to amp up the flavor. Top these crisp croquettes the traditional way, with ruby-colored beet horseradish, or simply squeeze a bit of lemon juice over the top. Either way, this might be the first year ever that half of your Passover guests don't send back their gefilte plates untouched.

2 TBSP VEGETABLE OIL, PLUS MORE FOR FRYING

1 LARGE ONION, FINELY CHOPPED

KOSHER SALT AND FRESHLY GROUND BLACK PEPPER

½ LB [225 G] SKINLESS SALMON FILLET, CUT INTO 1-IN [2.5-CM] CHUNKS

1½ LB [680 G] SKINLESS HALIBUT FILLET, CUT INTO 1-IN [2.5-CM] CHUNKS

3 EGGS, LIGHTLY BEATEN

2 CUPS [230 G] MATZO MEAL OR UNSEASONED PANKO BREAD CRUMBS

1 TSP ONION POWDER

½ TSP GARLIC POWDER

1 TSP DRIED THYME

1 TSP GRATED LEMON ZEST

¼ CUP [15 G] CHOPPED FRESH FLAT-LEAF PARSLEY

1. Heat 2 Tbsp vegetable oil in a medium skillet set over medium heat. Add the onion and a generous pinch of salt and cook, stirring occasionally, until softened and lightly browned, about 10 minutes. Remove from the heat and let cool to the touch.

2. Working in two batches, put the salmon and halibut in a food processor and pulse until finely chopped. The ground fish may appear a bit mushy—that is okay at this stage. Transfer the ground fish to a large bowl and add the sautéed onion, eggs, 1 cup [115 g] of the matzo meal, the onion powder, garlic powder, thyme, lemon zest, parsley, 1¼ tsp salt, and a generous amount of freshly ground

black pepper. Stir with a wooden spoon until well combined. Let sit for 30 minutes to allow the matzo meal to soften, or cover and store in the refrigerator overnight.

3. Line a large plate with a few layers of paper towels. Fill a large skillet with ¼ in [6 mm] of oil and heat over medium heat until shimmering. Spread the remaining 1 cup [115 g] matzo meal onto a separate plate and season with a little salt and pepper. Scoop out ¼ cup [60 g] of the fish mixture and form into patties about 3 in [7.5 cm] wide and ½ in [12 mm] thick. If the mixture is sticking to your hands, moisten them with a little water. Press each patty gently in the matzo meal, then turn to coat the other side.

4. Working in batches of 4 or 5, add the coated patties to the oil and cook until browned on one side, about 3 minutes; flip with a metal spatula and continue cooking on the other side until golden and cooked through, 2 to 3 minutes more. Adjust the heat if the patties are browning two quickly or not quickly enough and add more oil, if necessary.

5. Transfer the patties to prepared plate and let drain. Serve warm or at room temperature. Store leftovers, covered, in the refrigerator for up to 3 days. Reheat in an oven or toaster oven at 350°F [180°C] until warmed through, 10 to 15 minutes.

Potato and Red Onion Knishes

SERVES 8

A few years back, a food writing colleague and friend, Laura Silver, wrote a book called *Knish: In Search of the Jewish Soul Food*. Yes, that's right, an entire book dedicated to the knish, the squat pocket of dough filled with mashed potatoes, kasha, cabbage, curd cheese, or any number of hearty fillings. The Eastern European comfort food became a New York City classic, a warm, delightful gut bomb peddled by street vendors, in Jewish bakeries, and at Jewish delicatessens. Knishes can still be found at a few holdouts, like the more than a century-old Yonah Schimmel's Knish Bakery on Manhattan's Lower East Side. But, as Silver laments in the book, these days, a really good knish is hard to find—unless, of course, you make it yourself.

My version stays true to a classic mashed potato knish with a few tweaks, namely a scattering of poppy seeds in the dough for color and crunch, a generous amount of cream cheese mashed into the potatoes for over-the-top richness, and a splash of vermouth to give the caramelized onions sweetness and depth.

1½ CUPS [185 G] ALL-PURPOSE FLOUR

1 CUP [140 G] BREAD FLOUR

½ TSP BAKING POWDER

½ TSP KOSHER SALT

1 TBSP POPPY SEEDS

1 EGG

½ CUP [120 ML] WARM WATER

½ CUP [120 ML] VEGETABLE OIL

1 TSP APPLE CIDER VINEGAR

FILLING

1½ LB [680 G] RUSSET POTATOES, PEELED AND CUT INTO 2-IN [5-CM] CHUNKS

4 OZ [115 G] CREAM CHEESE

KOSHER SALT AND FRESHLY GROUND BLACK PEPPER

2 TBSP UNSALTED BUTTER

1 MEDIUM RED ONION, FINELY CHOPPED

1 TSP SUGAR

1 TBSP CHOPPED FRESH THYME

2 TBSP VERMOUTH (PAGE 127) OR DRY WHITE WINE

1 EGG, LIGHTLY BEATEN WITH 1 TBSP WATER

1. To make the dough: Whisk together the all-purpose flour, bread flour, baking powder, salt, and poppy seeds in a large bowl. In a small bowl, whisk together the egg, warm

water, oil, and vinegar. Make a well in the dry ingredients and pour in the wet ingredients. Stir until the dough comes together, then knead it a few times in the bowl with the heel of your hand and form it into a ball. Cover the bowl with plastic wrap and let sit at room temperature for at least 1 hour, or store in the refrigerator for up to 1 day.

2. Meanwhile, make the filling: Place the potatoes in a large saucepan. Cover with water by 2 in [5 cm] and set the pan over high heat. When the water boils, turn the heat to medium and cook until the potatoes are very tender, 10 to 15 minutes. Drain and transfer to a bowl. Add the cream cheese, 1 tsp salt, and a generous amount of black pepper and mash with a potato masher until creamy and well combined. Set aside.

3. Melt the butter in a medium skillet over medium heat. Add the onion, sugar, and a generous pinch of salt, cover, and cook until softened, about 10 minutes. Uncover, add 2 tsp water, turn the heat to medium-low, and continue to cook, stirring occasionally, until the onions are golden brown, 8 to 10 minutes. Add the thyme and vermouth and cook, stirring, until the vermouth evaporates, about 30 seconds. Remove from the heat. Fold the onion mixture into the mashed potatoes and let cool to the touch.

4. To assemble the knishes: Preheat the oven to 375°F [190°C] and line a large rimmed baking sheet with parchment paper. Cut the dough in half, returning one half back to the covered bowl while you work. Lay a large dish towel or tablecloth on a table and sprinkle generously with flour. Use a rolling pin to roll the dough as thinly as possible into a large rectangle, less than 1/8 in [4 mm] thick. Trim any ragged edges with a sharp knife. Take half of the potato mixture and use your hands to form it into a thick log. With the long side of the dough facing you, lay the potato log across the bottom edge of the dough. Roll the dough around the filling like a jelly roll. Repeat with the remaining dough and filling to make a second log. Trim the ends off each log so that they are flush with the filling.

5. Using the side of your hand (imagine a karate chop motion), make indentations along the log every 3 in [7.5 cm], then twist the dough at these points. Use a sharp knife to slice the dough at each twist, then pinch one side together to form the base of the knish. Flatten the knish a bit between your palms, then pinch together the tops to seal the filling inside the dough. Repeat with the remaining knishes. Lay the formed knishes on the prepared baking sheet and use two fingers to press a small indentation into the top of each one, which will keep them from opening during baking.

6. Brush the tops and sides of each knish with the egg wash (you won't use all of it). Bake the knishes, rotating the baking sheet halfway through cooking, until golden brown, about 45 minutes. Remove from the oven and let the knishes cool for at least 20 minutes. Serve warm or at room temperature. Cover leftovers tightly in plastic wrap and store in the refrigerator for up to 5 days or in the freezer for up to 3 months. Reheat in an oven or toaster oven at 350°F [180°C] until warmed through, 10 to 15 minutes.

Sweet Cheese and Fig Strudel

SERVES 8 TO 10

For centuries, strudel was considered the national dish of
the Austro-Hungarian Empire, and it continues to maintain
its powerful hold over Central European palates today.
Enjoyed by the wealthy and humble classes alike, the
process of hand stretching the dough to impossible thin-
ness, then rolling it with sweet (apple, cherry, poppy seed)
or savory (cabbage, mushroom, potato) fillings became a
regional art form. According to Gil Marks's *Encyclopedia
of Jewish Food*, "The ultimate quality of a housewife's
culinary skills was judged by her ability to make strudel
ausgezogen (pulled by hand)."

Strudel traveled to America with German Jews in the
mid-nineteenth century, where it became a staple at
Jewish bakeries and restaurants. Today, many strudel
recipes, mine included, swap in store-bought phyllo for
DIY dough. If you have the time and inclination to try
your hand at making your own dough, go for it! But I find
phyllo to be a worthy substitute.

While not difficult to make, this dish takes a bit of advance
planning. But the combination of cinnamon-perfumed
cheese and wine and honey-poached figs encased in
crackly, butter-rich phyllo makes it undeniably worth the
effort. Serve the strudel as is or with a dollop of sour cream
and an extra drizzle of honey.

1 CUP [240 G] RICOTTA CHEESE

3 OZ [85 G] CREAM CHEESE, AT ROOM TEMPERATURE

1 EGG YOLK

2 TABLESPOONS SUGAR

1 TSP VANILLA EXTRACT

1 TSP GROUND CINNAMON

¼ TSP KOSHER SALT

**¾ CUP [130 G] DRIED MISSION FIGS, STEMMED AND
FINELY CHOPPED**

¼ CUP [35 G] BLACK RAISINS

2 TABLESPOONS HONEY

¼ CUP ORANGE JUICE

½ CUP DRY RED WINE

¾ CUP [165 G] UNSALTED BUTTER

16 SHEETS THAWED FROZEN PHYLLO DOUGH

1. Spoon the ricotta into the center of a clean dish towel and squeeze out as much liquid as possible. Transfer the ricotta to a bowl and stir in the cream cheese, egg yolk, sugar, vanilla, cinnamon, and salt until smooth. Refrigerate until needed.

2. Meanwhile, combine the figs, raisins, honey, orange juice, and red wine in a small saucepan and set over medium-high heat. Bring to a boil, then turn heat to low and simmer, stirring occasionally and gently mashing the fruit with the back of a wooden spoon, until the figs are tender and liquid mostly evaporates, 10 to 15 minutes. Remove from heat and set aside to cool completely.

3. Preheat the oven to 400°F [200°C] and line a large baking sheet with parchment paper.

4. Melt the butter in a small pan set over low heat (or in the microwave). Lay a piece of parchment paper on a flat surface and place 1 piece of phyllo on top. (Cover the other phyllo pieces with a damp dish towel so they do not dry out.) Using a pastry brush, brush the sheet of phyllo all over with a thin layer of melted butter. Top with another sheet of phyllo and brush with butter; continue this pattern until you have a stack of 8 sheets of buttered phyllo. Reserve the remaining 8 sheets of phyllo.

5. Spoon half of the cheese mixture in a thick line along one of the short ends of the phyllo stack, leaving about 1/2 in [12 mm] of space along the edge. Layer half of the fig mixture on top of the cheese mixture. Use the parchment paper to help roll the dough around the filling, tucking the filling inside and ending up with a long, stuffed cylinder. Brush the top with more melted butter and carefully transfer to the prepared baking sheet. Repeat the process with the remaining 8 sheets of phyllo and butter (you can briefly reheat the butter if it cools and congeals too much to brush), and the remaining cheese mixture and fig mixture.

6. Bake strudels until golden, 20 to 30 minutes. Let cool to the touch, then use a serrated knife to cut into thick slices. Serve at room temperature.

Mushroom Piroshki

SERVES 6 TO 8

The word *pir* means "feast" in Russian and piroshki—one of many filled pastries found in Russian Jewish cuisine—are definitely little handheld feasts. Like most dumplings and turnovers, they can be filled with many things, both sweet and savory, but sautéed mushrooms are a beloved classic. I start with a sour cream-enriched dough and fill the savory pockets with a combination of cremini and shiitake mushrooms enhanced by chopped fresh herbs. These piroshki are the perfect size to serve alone as an appetizer, and excellent warmed up for an afternoon snack.

DOUGH

3 CUPS [380 G] ALL-PURPOSE FLOUR

½ TSP KOSHER SALT

1 TSP BAKING POWDER

½ CUP [115 G] COLD UNSALTED BUTTER, CUT INTO SMALL PIECES

2 EGGS

½ CUP [100 G] SOUR CREAM

FILLING

½ LB [225 G] RUSSET POTATOES, PEELED AND CUT INTO ½-IN [12-MM] PIECES

2 TBSP UNSALTED BUTTER

1 SMALL ONION, FINELY CHOPPED

KOSHER SALT AND FRESHLY GROUND BLACK PEPPER

½ LB [225 G] CREMINI MUSHROOMS, CLEANED WITH A PAPER TOWEL AND FINELY CHOPPED

¼ LB [115 G] SHIITAKE MUSHROOMS, CLEANED WITH A PAPER TOWEL AND FINELY CHOPPED

2 GARLIC CLOVES, MINCED OR PUSHED THROUGH A PRESS
1 TBSP FINELY CHOPPED FRESH THYME
1 TBSP FINELY CHOPPED FRESH SAGE

1 EGG, LIGHTLY BEATEN WITH 1 TBSP WATER

1. To make the dough: Combine the flour, salt, baking powder, butter, eggs, and sour cream in a food processor and process until the dough comes together as a ball, scraping down the sides of the processor bowl as necessary. Flatten the dough ball into a disk with your hands, cover in plastic wrap, and refrigerate for at least 30 minutes or up to 1 day.

2. Meanwhile, make the filling: Place the potato in a medium saucepan. Cover with water by 2 in [5 cm] and set the pan over high heat. When the water boils, turn the heat to medium and cook until the potato is very tender, 10 to 15 minutes. Drain and set aside.

3. Melt the butter in a large skillet over medium heat. Add the onion and a pinch of salt and cook, stirring occasionally, until the onion softens and begins to lightly brown, 7 to 8 minutes. Add the cremini and shiitake mushrooms and cook, stirring often, until the mushrooms are soft and most of their liquid evaporates, about 10 minutes. Add the garlic, thyme, sage, 1 tsp salt, and a generous amount of pepper and cook until fragrant, 1 to 2 minutes. Remove from the heat. Transfer the cooked potatoes to a large bowl

and mash with a potato masher until smooth. Stir in the mushroom mixture until well combined. (The filling can be stored, covered, in the refrigerator for up to 1 day.)

4. To assemble the piroshki: Preheat the oven to 400°F [200°C] and lightly butter two large rimmed baking sheets. Lay a large piece of parchment paper on a flat surface. Use a rolling pin to roll the dough as thinly as possible, less than 1/8 in [4 mm] thick. Use a 4-in [10-cm] cookie cutter to cut out as many rounds as possible.

5. Place a rounded Tbsp of filling in the center of each round of dough. Fold one side over to the other to form a half moon and press the edges of the dough to seal. Lay pastries on the prepared baking sheets, spacing them 1/2 in [12 mm] apart. Reroll the dough scraps and repeat the filling and folding process.

6. Brush the tops of each pastry with the egg wash (you won't use all of it). Bake the piroshki, rotating the baking sheet halfway through cooking, until golden brown, 20 to 25 minutes. Remove from the oven and transfer the baking sheets to cooling racks. Serve warm or at room temperature. Store leftovers, covered, in the refrigerator for up to 3 days or cover tightly in plastic wrap and store in the freezer for up to 3 months. Reheat in an oven or toaster oven at 350°F [180°C] until warmed through, 5 to 10 minutes.

Butternut Bichak

SERVES 8 TO 10

Bukharians are a truly unique community of Jews with ancient Persian roots who thrived along the Silk Road in Central Asia for more than two thousand years. Today, the Bukharian community mostly lives in Jerusalem and New York City. Their cuisine is made up of a delicious amalgam of dishes and flavors, with influences from Iran, Afghanistan, China, India, and Russia, among other places. Along with the cuisine's glistening lamb kebabs, hand-pulled noodle soups, and carrot- or cilantro-flecked pilafs are an impressive array of dumplings, turnovers, and hand pies.

One of my favorite Bukharian turnovers is bichak, a rustic yeast dough filled with mashed pumpkin and onions. My version turns up this basic flavor profile, starting with a base of butternut squash (which I find to be more readily available than pumpkin) and layering on a trifecta of sautéed shallots, fresh ginger, and garlic. I also like to add a bit of coconut oil for its rich, lightly sweet flavor, though vegetable oil works well too. Bichak are often served as a snack, and on Jewish holidays, but they would make a welcome addition to an appetizer platter. They also freeze well, so you can keep a batch on hand and pop them in the oven or toaster oven to warm up when guests come over.

2 TSP ACTIVE DRY YEAST

½ TSP SUGAR

1 CUP [240 ML] WARM WATER (ABOUT 110°F [43°C])

2½ CUPS [350 G] BREAD FLOUR, PLUS MORE AS NEEDED

1½ TSP KOSHER SALT

1 TBSP PLUS 2 TSP VEGETABLE OIL

FILLING

1½ LB [680 G] BUTTERNUT SQUASH, HALVED LENGTHWISE AND SEEDS SCOOPED OUT

2 TBSP UNREFINED COCONUT OIL OR VEGETABLE OIL

2 MEDIUM SHALLOTS, FINELY CHOPPED

KOSHER SALT AND FRESHLY GROUND BLACK PEPPER

ONE 2-IN [5-CM] PIECE GINGER, PEELED AND GRATED ON THE LARGE HOLES OF A BOX GRATER

4 GARLIC CLOVES, MINCED OR PUSHED THROUGH A PRESS

1 TSP SUGAR

1 EGG, LIGHTLY BEATEN WITH 1 TBSP WATER

1. Stir together the yeast, sugar, and warm water in a medium bowl. Let sit until foaming, 5 to 10 minutes.

2. In a large bowl, stir together the flour and salt. Stir 1 Tbsp of the vegetable oil into the yeast mixture, then pour into the flour. Stir until the dough starts to come together, then turn out onto a floured surface and knead, adding a little more flour, if needed, until the dough is smooth and

elastic but not sticky, 8 to 10 minutes. (You can also knead the dough in a standing mixer fit with the dough hook on medium speed for 5 to 8 minutes.)

3. Pour the remaining 2 tsp oil into a large bowl, add the dough, and turn to coat. Cover the bowl with plastic wrap or a damp dish towel and leave in a warm place until it doubles in size, 1 to 1 1/2 hours.

4. Meanwhile, make the filling: Preheat the oven to 400°F [200°C] and line a large rimmed baking sheet with aluminum foil. Place the squash, cut side down, on the baking sheet and roast until tender and a knife can be easily inserted into the flesh, 40 to 50 minutes. Remove from the oven and use a pair of tongs to flip over the squash. Let cool to the touch, then scoop the flesh into a medium bowl, discarding the skin, and mash with a potato masher until smooth. (The squash can be stored, covered, in the refrigerator for up to 2 days.)

5. Heat the coconut oil in a medium pan set over medium-low heat. Add the shallots and a pinch of salt and cook, stirring often, until softened, 5 to 6 minutes. Add the ginger, garlic, and sugar and cook, stirring, until fragrant, 1 to 2 minutes. Remove from the heat and season with salt and pepper to taste. Stir the shallot mixture into the mashed squash until well combined.

6. To assemble the bishak: Turn the oven to 350°F [180°C] and line two large rimmed baking sheets with parchment paper. Gently deflate the dough with the palm of your hand and turn out onto a lightly floured surface. Cut the dough in half, returning one half to the covered bowl while you work. Use a rolling pin to roll the dough as thinly as possible, less than ⅛ in [4 mm] thick. Use a 3-in [7.5 cm] cookie cutter to cut out as many rounds as possible.

7. Place a heaping teaspoon of squash filling in the center of each round of dough. To close the dough over the filling, bring four corners up to create a pyramid shape and pinch them to seal, forming square or rectangular pies. Reroll the dough scraps and repeat the filling and forming process.

8. Place the pastries on the prepared baking sheets. Brush the tops with the egg wash (you won't use all of it). Bake the bichak until golden brown, 20 to 25 minutes. Remove from the oven and transfer the baking sheets to cooling racks. Serve warm or at room temperature. Store leftovers, covered, in the refrigerator for up to 3 days or cover tightly in plastic wrap and store in the freezer for up to 3 months. Reheat in an oven or toaster oven at 350°F [180°C] until warmed through, 5 to 10 minutes.

Spinach Bulemas

MAKES 15 TO 18

Sephardi Jewish cuisine is renowned for its savory pastries, with bourekas being the most popular example. But bulemas, a yeasted pastry that is spiraled into a plump coil and usually filled with spinach and cheese or eggplant and cheese, are worth getting to know. My version skews fairly traditional, though I could not resist adding a hint of fresh basil. The dough for bulemas differs from most yeast doughs I have worked with in that it rests in a substantial oil bath as it rises. The oil makes the dough wonderfully supple and easy to roll out. As the bulemas bake, the slick of residual oil creates a crackly outer shell that encases the tender pastry and savory filling inside. Serve bulemas the traditional way, with a glass of arak to sip between bites. Or pack them into a lunch box for the perfect afternoon snack.

DOUGH

1½ TSP ACTIVE DRY YEAST

1 TSP SUGAR

1 CUP [240 ML] WARM WATER (ABOUT 110°F [43°C])

2½ CUPS [350 G] BREAD FLOUR, PLUS MORE AS NEEDED

1½ TSP KOSHER SALT

⅓ CUP [75 ML] PLUS 1 TBSP VEGETABLE OIL

2 TBSP VEGETABLE OIL

2 MEDIUM SHALLOTS, HALVED THROUGH THE ROOT AND THINLY SLICED

KOSHER SALT AND FRESHLY GROUND BLACK PEPPER

5 OZ [140 G] BABY SPINACH, FINELY CHOPPED

20 FRESH BASIL LEAVES, CHOPPED

1½ CUPS [150 G] CRUMBLED FETA CHEESE

⅓ CUP [10 G] FINELY GRATED PARMESAN CHEESE

1 EGG, LIGHTLY BEATEN WITH 1 TBSP WATER

1. Stir together the yeast, sugar, and warm water in a medium bowl. Let sit until foaming, 5 to 10 minutes.

2. In a large bowl, stir together the flour and salt. Stir 1 Tbsp of the vegetable oil into the yeast mixture, then pour into the flour. Stir until the dough starts to come together, then turn out onto a floured surface and knead, adding a little more flour, if needed, until the dough is smooth and elastic but not sticky, 8 to 10 minutes. (You can also knead the dough in a standing mixer fit with the dough hook on medium speed for 5 to 8 minutes.)

3. Pour the remaining ⅓ cup [75 ml] oil into a large shallow baking dish. Divide the dough into 15 to 20 equal pieces and roll into balls. Place the balls in the oil and turn to coat. Cover the baking dish and let sit in a warm place until the dough swells, about 30 minutes.

4. Meanwhile, make the filling: Heat the oil in a medium saucepan set over medium heat. Add the shallots and a pinch of salt and cook, stirring occasionally, until softened and lightly browned, 5 to 6 minutes. Remove from the heat and let cool to the touch. In a large bowl, stir together the cooled shallots, the spinach, basil, feta, Parmesan, and a generous amount of black pepper.

5. To assemble the bulemas: Preheat the oven to 375°F [190°C] and line two large baking sheets with parchment paper. Lay another piece of parchment paper on a flat surface. Working with one ball of dough at a time, place the ball on top of the parchment. Use your fingertips and a rolling pin to stretch and roll into very thin, 9-in [23-cm] diameter rounds. Spread 2 rounded Tbsp of filling in a line along the edge of one side of the dough round. Roll up the dough tightly like a jelly roll, starting with the filled side; gently stretch the roll with your fingertips to lengthen slightly. Starting from one end of the roll, coil it onto itself, tucking the end underneath.

6. Place the coiled pastries on the prepared baking sheets and brush with the egg wash (you won't use all of it). Bake until golden brown, 30 to 40 minutes. Remove from the oven and transfer the baking sheets to cooling racks. Serve warm or at room temperature. Store leftovers in an airtight container in the refrigerator for up to 1 week or in the freezer for up to 3 months. Reheat in an oven or toaster oven at 350°F [180°C] until warmed through, 5 to 10 minutes.

Lahmajun

Jews hailing from Syria, Turkey, Lebanon, and surrounding countries took the lead from their neighbors and fell in love with these small flatbreads topped with ground lamb or beef. The name is quite literal, stemming from a contraction of the Arabic words *laham b'ajin* or "meat with dough." The yeasted dough is rolled quite thin and crisps around the edges while baking. The topping, meanwhile, is enriched with fragrant spices and pine nuts that add subtle flavor and crunch. Drizzle the lahmajun with good-quality tahini and shower it with fresh parsley and lemon juice, then slice into wedges and serve as a decadent party or dinner appetizer.

DOUGH

1¼ OZ [7 G] PACKAGE ACTIVE DRY YEAST (2¼ TSP)

1 TSP SUGAR

¾ CUP [180 ML] WARM WATER (ABOUT 110°F [43°C])

2 CUPS [255 G] ALL-PURPOSE FLOUR, PLUS MORE AS NEEDED

1½ TSP KOSHER SALT

1 TBSP PLUS 1 TSP EXTRA-VIRGIN OLIVE OIL

2 TBSP EXTRA-VIRGIN OLIVE OIL

4 GARLIC CLOVES, MINCED OR PUSHED THROUGH A PRESS

1 PLUM TOMATO, SEEDED AND FINELY CHOPPED

KOSHER SALT

½ LB [225 G] GROUND LAMB OR BEEF

½ SMALL ONION, GRATED ON THE LARGE HOLES OF A BOX GRATER

1 TSP SWEET PAPRIKA

¼ TSP RED PEPPER FLAKES

¼ TSP GROUND CINNAMON

½ TSP GROUND CUMIN

1 TSP ZA'ATAR (PAGE 128)

1 TBSP TOMATO PASTE

¼ CUP [40 G] PINE NUTS

CHOPPED FRESH FLAT-LEAF PARSLEY, TAHINI, AND LEMON WEDGES FOR SERVING

1. To make the dough: Stir together the yeast, sugar, and warm water in a medium bowl. Let sit until foaming, 5 to 10 minutes.

2. In a large bowl, stir together the flour and salt. Stir in 1 Tbsp of the olive oil into the yeast mixture, then pour into the flour. Stir until the dough starts to come together, then turn out onto a lightly floured surface and knead, adding

a little more flour, if needed, until the dough is smooth and elastic but not sticky, 7 to 8 minutes. (You can also knead the dough in a standing mixer fit with the dough hook on medium speed for 5 to 7 minutes.)

3. Pour the remaining 1 tsp of oil into a large bowl, add the dough, and turn to coat. Cover the bowl with a damp dish towel and leave in a warm place until it doubles in size, about 1 hour. Gently deflate the dough with the palm of your hand and turn out onto a lightly floured surface. Cut the dough into four equal portions and roll each portion into a ball. Transfer the dough balls to a floured baking sheet. Cover with a damp dish towel and let rest in a warm place until soft and pliable, 30 to 45 minutes.

4. Meanwhile, make the filling: Heat the olive oil in a medium skillet set over medium heat. Add the garlic, tomato, and a pinch of salt and cook, stirring occasionally, until softened, 5 to 7 minutes. Remove from the heat and set aside to cool. Stir together the lamb, onion, paprika, red pepper flakes, cinnamon, cumin, za'atar, 1 tsp salt, tomato paste, pine nuts, and cooled tomatoes in a large bowl. Mix together with your hands until well combined.

5. Preheat the oven to 450°F [230°C] and line two large rimmed baking sheets with parchment paper. Lay another piece of parchment on a flat surface. Working with one ball of dough at a time, place the ball on top of the parchment. Use a rolling pin to roll the dough into a 8-in [20-cm] circle. Lay the dough on the prepared baking sheet, top with one quarter of the topping (the meat should still be raw), and use your fingers to press it evenly to the edges. Sprinkle with a little salt. Repeat with remaining dough and topping.

6. Bake until the dough is golden brown and topping is cooked through, 15 to 18 minutes. Remove from oven and let cool slightly. Slice into wedges and sprinkle with parsley and drizzle with tahini. Serve warm, with lemon wedges on the side for squeezing.

PAIRING IDEAS

UPDATED FORSPEIS SPREAD

The classic Eastern European Shabbat appetizer consists of a slice of horseradish-topped gefilte fish, a schmear of chopped liver, or perhaps a little bite of schmaltz herring. This *forspeis* (Yiddish for appetizer) menu is inspired by tradition, but with a few welcome twists.

Fried Gefilte Fish (page 84)

Chopped Egg and Caramelized Onion Spread (page 12)

Vegetarian Chopped Liver with Shallots (page 15)

Pickled Cherry Tomatoes (page 52)

Everything-Spice Rye Crackers (page 39)

MIDDLE EASTERN MEZZE SPREAD

Sumptuous Middle Eastern mezze spreads often include more than a dozen dips, spreads, salads, and little bites—all before the actual meal is served! Here are seven of my favorites.

Green Matbucha (page 26)

Smoky Sweet Potato Hummus (page 19)

Muhammara (page 29)

Za'atar-Garlic Pita Chips (page 43)

Beet-Pickled Turnips (page 55)

Moroccan Orange and Black Olive Salad (page 36)

Lahmajun (page 113)

118

ELEGANT DINNER PARTY HORS D'OEUVRES

Pop open a bottle of something sparkly to serve alongside these dressed-up apps.

Smoked Trout Canapés (page 51)

Borscht Crostini (page 46)

Eggplant Carpaccio (page 23)

Moroccan Orange and Black Olive Salad (page 36)

Butternut Bichak (page 103)

Persian Zucchini and Herb Frittata (page 68)

COCKTAIL PARTY

These one-bite dishes and sultry spreads are perfect for nibbling with one hand while holding a cocktail in the other.

Albóndigas (page 80)

Fried Artichoke Hearts (page 73)

Shiitake and Scallion Falafel (page 75)

Smoky Sweet Potato Hummus (page 19)

Muhammara (page 29)

Za'atar-Garlic Pita Chips (page 43)

HANUKKAH PARTY APPETIZERS

Keep holiday guests sated with these substantial snacks and dips while you fry up the next batch of latkes.

Smoked Trout Canapés (page 51)

Barley-Stuffed Mushrooms (page 65)

Persian Zucchini and Herb Frittata (page 68)

Perfect Tzatziki (page 33)

Sweet Cheese and Fig Strudel (page 94)

A Jewish Cheese Plate (page 58)

Everything-Spice Rye Crackers (page 39) or Za'atar-Garlic Pita Chips (page 43)

SURPRISE VISITOR SNACKS

Store a batch of these treats in your freezer at all times and pop them in the oven or toaster oven whenever unexpected guests arrive, or if you are craving an out-of-the ordinary snack.

Potato and Red Onion Knishes (page 89)

Spinach Bulemas (page 107)

Shiitake and Scallion Falafel (page 75)

Mushroom Piroshki (page 99)

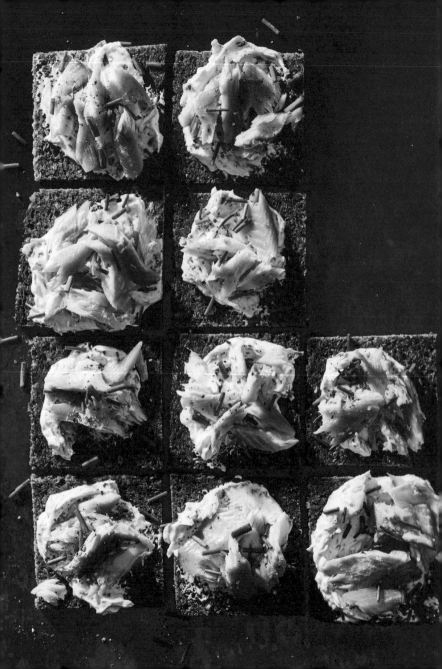

INGREDIENT GLOSSARY
AND SOURCES

Having difficulty finding an ingredient at your local supermarket? Harness the power of online shopping and the ingredient you need will be delivered right to your door.

Artisanal Cheese

The landscape of kosher-certified artisanal cheese has grown in the last decade. When putting together a Jewish cheese plate (page 58), consider adding a wedge from the following kosher-certified artisanal creameries: 5 Spoke Creamery in New York state, Narragansett Creamery in Rhode Island, and Redwood Hill Farm & Creamery in California. 5spokecreamery.com / Richeeses.com / Redwoodhill.com

Chickpea Flour

Also known as garbanzo bean flour, this gluten-free, high-protein flour is made from ground raw or roasted chickpeas. Bob's Red Mill makes a flavorful stone-ground version that serves as the perfect binder for Shiitake and Scallion Falafel (page 75). Bobsredmill.com

Harissa Paste

Harissa is a Tunisian hot sauce made from a variety of chile peppers. I am in love with NYShuk's version, which is smoky and chocolaty, with just the right amount of gentle heat. Piquant also makes a kosher-certified version that adds nice flavor to Shiitake and Scallion Falafel (page 75) and Albóndigas (page 80). NYshuk.com / Sahadis.com

Oil-Cured Black Olives

I grew up eating—or rather refusing, because I was picky—canned black olives that came floating in brine. As an adult, I discovered the oil-cured variety—black olives that are dry-cured in salt and then soaked in oil. The ink-black, wrinkly, glistening little beauties add a ton of flavor to Moroccan Orange and Black Olive Salad (page 36). Pastene makes a very worthy kosher-certified version. Store.pastene.com

Pomegranate Molasses

Used throughout the Middle East, pomegranate molasses, which is essentially pomegranate juice reduced to a thick syrup, adds tartness to Muhammara (page 29). Golchin makes a lovely, kosher-certified version. You can also make your own: Boil down 1 cup [240 ml] of pomegranate juice in a small pan set over medium heat, stirring occasionally, until it turns thick and syrupy, 10 to 15 minutes. Persianbasket.com

Smoked Trout

Smoked trout is trout that gets brined and then hot-smoked over wood, resulting in a flaky, mild fish that is an hors d'oeuvres' best friend. It can be found in specialty food stores alongside the lox and herring and is the perfect topper for canapés (page 51). Rachael's Springfield Smoked Fish also makes a delicious version that can be shipped directly to your door. Rachaelsfoodcorp.com

Tahini

The ground sesame paste is fairly easy to find today in both specialty food stores and supermarkets. But I am partial to the version made by Soom Foods. Made from Ethiopian white humera sesame seeds, it is delicate and rich and just the thing to blend into Smoky Sweet Potato Hummus (page 19) or drizzle on top of Eggplant Carpaccio (page 23). Soomfoods.com

Vermouth

Kedem makes a kosher-certified version of this fortified wine, which comes flavored with roots, bark, spices, and other botanicals. Royalwine.com

Za'atar

Za'atar is a fragrant herb that grows in the Middle East and also the name of a spice mixture that includes that herb, along with sesame seeds, ground sumac, and salt. Teeny Tiny Spice Company makes a delicious version. teenytinyspice.com

ACKNOWLEDGMENTS

This book may be little in size, but my gratitude for everyone who helped bring it to life is huge.

Thanks, as always, to my agent, Jenni Ferrari-Adler, for her ongoing support and advice. And thanks to my editor Sarah Billingsley, design director Vanessa Dina, and the whole talented team at Chronicle Books.

I'm amazed and awed by the photography team's work. Linda Pugliese, Carrie Purcell, Paige Hicks, Levi Miller: you are incredible.

Thank you to the many friends and family members who volunteered to test recipes in their own home kitchens, and who sent me priceless feedback. In no particular order (because they are all equally great!):

Ahuva Hanau, Tiffany Mei, Alexandra Kuperman, Marti Reinfeld and Ilde Burgos, Magdalena Hutter and Jespa Kleinfeld, Marjorie Ingall and Jonathan Steuer, Rebecca and David Rendsburg, Shira Kohn, David Wolkin and Keeli Sorensen, Hean Zeidner Kaspi, Elisheva Margulies, Stephen Klein, Rev. Martha Koenig Stone, Miriam Bader, Rabbi Barat Ellman, Georgia and Josh Freedman-Wand, Rabbi Aaron Finkelstein and Julie Sugar, Rachel Weston, Lindsey Paige, Jenny Levison, Carol Koenig, Temim Fruchter and Oliver Bendorf, Ora Fruchter and Bradford Jordan, Dasi Fruchter, Benjy Fox-Rosen and Julie Dawson, Shayn Smulyan, and Noa Heyman.

A million thank yous to my mom, Carol, my in-laws, Rena and Chaim, and my ever-expanding sibling tribe: Seth and Sara, Temim and Oliver, Ora and Bradford, and Maharat Dasi, for their love, wisdom, and encouragement.

And finally, big love and thanks to my guys, both large and small: to Yoshie for being my number one taste tester, support, and listening ear. And to Max, for loving all the pickles.

INDEX